AF430277

*This book is dedicated to my husband and children who live
with this hot mess. They are my rock, my calm, and my world.*

INTRODUCTION

I can't be depressed; I was laughing with my family last night!

Now, I don't know how many people with depression have uttered this phrase, but it definitely came out of my mouth. Depressed people don't laugh, they might try and crack a smile, but laughing, no that's not part of it… Is it?

This book will delve into the past few years of my life, taking in thoughts, actions, why's, how's and eventually the understanding of what the heck was going on inside my head.

I hope that my take on depression will ring true, will make you think, will give you understanding and hopefully, if needed, lead you to people that can help. Or, if you recognise these things in other people you love, work with them to guide them to help.

My wish is that, as you read my light-hearted view on this condition, you will understand that although smiles are on the surface, they hide a depth of feelings beneath.

Read on, enjoy, and embrace my depression and all that comes with it!

CONTENTS

Can't shake it

Recognition

Master of fine architecture

CBT, nope, not your bike test!

Places

Walking Hand in Hand

Where to now

CAN'T SHAKE IT

I've always loved the feeling of making people laugh. It is a great sense of joy to me, I was taught…" Leave people better than you found them". This I tried to make my mission in life. I enjoyed it, the feeling of coming away from someone having made them laugh or even just having brought a smile to their face made my day. So, when that feeling started to fade within me, I couldn't understand why.

What was going on, was I becoming selfish with my time, I'm a mum of six, I was working in Primary education, and working with special needs children, who had high needs. I was exhausted coming home, as soon as I walked out of work, I switched straight into mum mode and everything that entails. At church I was over-seeing the youth, which meant a lesson being taught every Sunday. On top of that everything else that life kindly passes you on a platter.

Don't get me wrong, I loved every part of my life, I felt I was doing okay in all parts, but I just couldn't shake this feeling I had. I later went on to find out I had high functioning depression, I was told it is the most exhausting one, due to multi-tasking, life, emotions, physical and mental. High functioning will generally allow people to go about their daily lives, work, fulfil daily duties and responsibilities all while dealing with depression (I kept saying I was the master multitasker, and everybody scoffed).

Something else I was told was that High Functioning normally heightens feelings of failure due to the high unachievable levels of perfection that the individual puts on themselves. Therefore, feeling worthless and a failure. All of this coupled by the need of validation from peers, well, it's a recipe for disaster. Trying to maintain a life on both sides of the mask is not going to work and will eventually put so much pressure on the individual's mental health, that a breaking point is inevitable.

Things happen in life that bring you down for a while, but you bounce back, revived and ready for the next thing. In 2016, maybe even a bit before, I realised I wasn't bouncing back as quick. It was harder to come back smiling. This wasn't me. I am totally an overthinker, to my detriment but this was different. All I could say was, "I don't know, I just can't shake this feeling".

I'll skip forward (because you really don't need my life history) to when I believe it ramped up a notch.

Now I can get emotional, a film, an advert, a book, or watching my children; but man, I was crying and not knowing why. I was dehydrated. I felt sorry my husband. I just kept thinking; the poor guy had to work then come home to this crazy mess. I stopped wearing mascara for a while as I looked like Marilyn Manson some days upon his return. He really didn't need that as a welcome. In fact, it's just come to me as I write... there is waterproof mascara!!! Anyways, it was getting to a point where I was exhausted from the day, and then on top of that, exhausted from whatever was going on inside me.

I was tired on all fronts.

But do you know what I did, instead of talking to someone, I looked at other women, saw that they were holding down jobs, families, church callings, and a social life, and thought.......... What's wrong with me, I must be weak, I'm struggling to do this and I'm crying all the time. Big fat failure. The fat I would find out in a year or two would be true.

Why do we do this? Compare, compare, compare. Looking back now it frustrates me, but I didn't know better, so I didn't do better. Living is learning, you never stop learning till you stop living. I hope to be learning for quite a while longer. As well as jumping out of a plane on my 80th birthday; I did it on my 40th, so I thought every forty years was good. I digress, sorry.

Now I'm surrounded by some pretty amazing women, each amazing in the pathway they have chosen and they absolutely rock their areas, so when you're in the start of (as I now know) depression, this can be quite overwhelming trying to keep up.

A little side note, you may think you've got it all under control when you turn up having spent hours the previous day choosing what you and the rest of the family will wear, having remembered to put petrol in the car, having a smile on your face the whole time and speaking to your kids like one of the Stepford wives, but if you're sat there the whole time worrying what people are thinking of you, overthinking every little conversation you had throughout the day and what they meant by it, you don't have it under control!!!

Yep, welcome to my world. An overthinker with depression and anxiety. I laugh as I write so I don't break the laptop with my tears, but do you know what, I'm starting to fall in love with life again, and I'll let you know how that has come to be.

RECOGNITION

There comes a time when you are so far down a hole that you need someone else to throw down a ladder and guide you towards it, because it's too dark to see where the ladder even is. Once you've found it, you look up to see the tiny speck of light at the top, the person at the top will shout to you to feel for the first step, you feel like you're going lower because you're bending down on your knees, fumbling around to find it, going at it like crazy because you're scared of the dark, they shout out to be methodical, to feel for one side of the ladder, then calmly from there, feel for the first step, once you find it, they then say to step onto it.

This can be scary in itself, putting all your faith in something you can't see, but you tentatively put your weight on the first step and lift yourself towards the pinprick of light. As you listen to their voice, and gradually gain confidence in the ladder you realise you're getting closer to the exit, but then you realise you have grown used to the darkness and suddenly become fearful of the light. You hesitate for a moment, but as you stay there for a minute, feeling the light on your face, you recognise that you came from light, and that this feels good.

You can liken this to what happens when you finally find out, come to the conclusion, or are told, that you have depression.

Listening to and working with others is what will finally help you to get out of it. But it's scary making those first steps. You have to acknowledge that you have something wrong with you, and to make it worse, it's linked to mental health. 'People will think I'm crazy and treat me differently'. To be fair, everyone has some form of mental health issue, so no big deal.

Taking care of your mental health is just as important as taking care of your physical health, we see our bodies every day, we don't see our brains, so that's why we forget! Plus sometimes, we as humans are very clever at hiding mental health, people will see a plaster or a broken leg and know what to do, a mind is not so easy to see, therefore not easy for others to know how to handle. Can't blame them, I don't know sometimes how to handle myself.

My first time of thinking I might have depression was sat on my sofa, I just had a feeling to google (yep google has the answers to everything in life) symptoms of depression. I picked the first thing that came up, it had a list of 25 things, I ticked off 24. That hit me like a ton of bricks but focussing on the one I didn't have bought some blessed relief. Look for silver linings! I mulled it over for a while, then decided that google wasn't a doctor and left it. So, this must have been in 2017 at some point, I'm the world's worst journal keeper, if I need to see what year something was, I go to my Instagram account! So 2017, I felt life absolutely hammering me, trying to come up for air but being pushed down again.

I must point out at this point it wasn't all woe is me. I had, and still have, a husband who loved me, 6 great children, a job, a nice home (rented, but now have bought in an area we love), family and friends around me, financially good, and some amazing travel.

Depression doesn't happen because bad things happen around you or your life is bad, it clings to all sorts of people, it doesn't care about money, class, religion, colour, it works its way in and sits and grows. I actually said to my husband I felt like a brat, I have this, and I still feel this way.

Now, Grant (my husband) is not one to beat around the bush, and

I thought he was going to agree, but he simply said, "you've not been you for a while". Let the crying commence, I just sat and cried, and he said he thought I should try to do something about it, I agreed, knowing in the back of my mind I was already popping it away into that box in your brain, that you put stuff in that you don't want to deal with yet. This is what I mean about having faith in the person trying to help, listening to their guidance on trying to find that first step.

So, 2017-2019 held a lot in store for me (family as well, but this book is about me, just in case we forget).

Grant's mum had not long died, and two more deaths came along, my Aunt and my cousin's beautiful son. My youngest daughter, who was 11 years of age at the time, was diagnosed very suddenly with Type 1 Diabetes.

This looking back was very traumatic, everything happened so suddenly, one minute at home, the next in the high dependency unit at the hospital. We moved house, same area, but the house we had bought was a total doer upper. Grant was travelling a lot at the time, so he'd work on it when he was home doing all the major bits, and the kids and I would come home from work and school, have dinner and go straight round to fill, sand, paint, wash, rip out at the house (we've learned an important lesson, always give yourselves a few weeks cross over when buying houses, makes the move a lot easier).

As all this was happening, I was taking the hit, and not getting up again. It saw all areas of my life suffering. I wasn't giving work 100%, I started pulling away from family and friends (I'll speak more about this later), I wasn't spending quality time with my children, I would take myself to my room so I didn't have to deal with things, I would cook dinner and disappear. I am a massive fan of my bed too, so this didn't help.

All of this happening with no knowledge and understanding. That's scary, and to be honest, pretty crap. So I.... nope, I didn't cry this time... I shut myself away emotionally, and probably, others would say, physically.

I just want to elaborate on the quality time with my children. I look around the world today and see parents with their children. Some have smiles on their faces, some look close to tears, some look like they'd rather be somewhere else, but all of these parents are with their children…Physically!!

Where are they mentally with them?

I find it interesting now as I have been through a time of not being mentally present for my kids to know if people are present in both ways or just physically?

From the outside you are doing your job, You've done what Mum's (or Dad's) are doing all over the world, you've made breakfast, you've done the school run, you've come home, tidied (this takes great energy and willpower), you remember to pick your kids up from school, you cook them dinner and then your mental presence can't do anymore, it's exhausted.

Your kids want to talk, want you to do stuff, so you think 'if I'm physically present that will do'. Don't get me wrong, you're there, and if that's all you can do, be physically present, my kids could talk to me (I became a good listener), they could cuddle up to me and they could show me what they deemed necessary for me to see, but I wasn't engaging with them, I would give the odd response and hope that was enough.

We beat ourselves up as parents as it is, 'Did I do enough?' 'Should I have handled that better?' 'Did I give my kids enough confidence to go out into the world?' So, whack Depression on top of that, enter stage left…. Guilt. You seem to carry guilt around in the pocket of the cloak of depression.

Depression doesn't make you blind, you see exactly what is happening in your life, you just have no control over it. It's frustrating at times.

I felt at least I was there for my kids to see, but there were times I would cook dinner and then announce "I'm really tired today,

I'm going to go lay on my bed for a while", these were the day's I wasn't handling life well, my thinking was, if I took myself away, the kids wouldn't be affected. They wouldn't have to deal with a broken Mum.

Reading the quote back to myself makes me sound like the Queen of Sheba, I'm really not that dramatic, unless I'm about to get a parking ticket, then all my high school drama classes rise up to the challenge!!

So, by elaborating on this point, I just wanted to point out that if you are just being physically present with your kids, try not to feel guilty, but also recognise it as a sign that something may not be being handled very well inside. A little help sign from under the cloak may be handy for others to know that they need to step in and help lift that cloak off before it becomes too heavy.

Think of it this way....

One day you feel a bit tired, you feel as though you're carrying something on your back, you're not sure what because you can't see back there. This would be a perfect time to say to someone 'could you just get whatever that is off my back please'. You don't though, Why? You're embarrassed!

You're not sure what it is, and if the other person can see it, you think they'll laugh and makes fun, so you keep quiet. You plod on, but this thing gets heavier, and starts to envelope you, it starts to close off your vision, so you can't see if there is anyone to help.

This also would be a good time to ask for help. The thing on your back gets bigger and heavier, so instead of one person being able to remove it, you'll need more.

You're still embarrassed though, because now your vision is marred, you don't want to call out and no one is there, and you look like a fool. So you walk on, all the time, your back becoming more weighed down by the day. Then one day, someone see's you crushed on the floor underneath the growth and needs to ask a team of others to help remove it.

How much better would it have been to just ask the one person at the beginning to take it off, saving all that time and energy. How easy it sounds; how incredibly hard it is to do. That's why surrounding yourself with people who know and love you is the best way to come through this soul-destroying time.

With the recognition of depression and anxiety comes the recognition of who you are as an individual. Let me enlighten you to my findings about myself, good and bad, funny and sad. (As you can see, I have become a poet throughout this time!)

I don't think doing it chronologically will work as I don't remember when I discovered these things, I just know I did, so please take that in to account as you read, saves me explaining the messed up scrap yard that is my brain!!

I found that I was actually quite pessimistic, the bad was happening, why wouldn't it continue to happen? I'm not one to ask for help, I've always been like this, even before depression, I think I can handle things on my own.

I do fail at things, but that's ok. I can be selfish, 'I really don't want to do something'; 'I really can't do something'; 'Don't make me do this'; (otherwise known as self-preservation at this time).

I'm actually really forgetful, this is a sign of depression, but also a quality I think I have. I have to write things down in my diary or they don't happen. (I have a magic diary).

I overthink, I wish that one would stop. I worry what people think of me, and it's always negative in my mind, but… I'm a trier, I'll give things a go, unless it has anything to do with snakes or mice, then I'm outta there.

I do have strength, under the weight I was carrying, I managed to go on, I lifted a weight I didn't think I could ever physically lift.

I love people, I love interaction, I love human nature, I love hugs, I'm a hugger, I gauge a lot by hugs! I am willing (sometimes with eyes shut) to see my flaws, recognise what needs to change and try to work on it.

I've found that the ideal of perfection doesn't exist on this earth, that's what we're all striving for, but nobody expects me to be perfect (well some do, and I just ignore them now!!)

I've found the joy in life again, finding happiness in the small areas of life, a sunrise or sunset do it for me, nature's palette is hard to beat.

I love laughter, I love the laughter that makes you cry, and your belly hurt. I didn't laugh enough during those years, and I'm sad about that.

I remembered that family relationships (and friendships that feel like family) were essential, Family is everything. Whatever your family circumstances are, if you are close or you have no family, make one. Find people that will become your family and will want to be in your life to make it better. Everyone needs a family.

Something that has just occurred to me as I write is that throughout my life I listened to other people that were having a hard time, that felt low, that felt worthless, and I would always try to make them feel of their worth, let them know that they are always worthy of being loved, thought of, served, talked to.

Why then, when it came to my own worthiness, was it different? Why was my worth any less than those people I would talk to? Why couldn't I feel that self-love?

I believe a lot of factors played a part, but as I write my experiences, I believe that a lot of it had to do with my moments in life and the way I had handled them.

I had to think back over my life to try to pinpoint times I thought had contributed. This was hard, as I had a wonderful childhood, obviously there were the usual things outside the home, school can be a breeding ground for insecurity and lack of confidence. But as I started to think, things popped into my mind.

Reflection can sometimes be hard but worth every pondered second. It can bring back unwanted feelings, but also the joy of triumph over certain situations. (just don't turn it into overthinking!!). This I found quite helpful to know, it showed me from where some of these feelings had started. Having a starting point is always helpful.

Through everything I never lost my desire for adventure and need to travel. I often wonder why, when most of my senses were dulled these two things burned just as bright as they always had. I've come to this conclusion.

As soon as I started packing, an excitement would start to build in me, at the airport I would hand over my passport, they would see my face was the same and my name, but they didn't know me and what was inside, travel gave me the opportunity to be the Keely I wanted back.

I left the broken me I so desperately wanted to fix behind, and through that passport gate walked a whole me.

Travel made me whole again, even if for a couple of weeks. I was in a place (or many places as it is with our travel) where I didn't have to say I was fine, deal with things that were crippling me, or try to pretend. I felt light, I felt free, I often asked if we could stay.

But I guess running away from your problems to some hot idyllic place, with the bluest sky and sea is not the way to deal with things.

MASTER OF FINE ARCHITECTURE

I didn't quite see myself doing it in the beginning but towards the end it was brutally obvious. I'd built a 'fine' house. What's building houses got to do with depression I hear you say, let me enlighten you as it has a lot to do with it.

When you are completely oblivious to what may be developing inside you, you learn to manage life with coping mechanisms that are easy and keep so-called problems at bay. Mine was the word 'Fine'.

"How are you?"   Fine

"How did the morning go with so and so?"   Fine

"How's things going at home?" Fine

"You look tired, how are you feeling?" Fine

That was my go-to word, and kept people where I needed them, enough away from me so they couldn't see how broken I felt. That way I didn't put them in a position where they felt like they had to help. There was one person who never believed the word fine, but I'll come back to her later.

If I can get your imaginations going for a minute. Hopefully as children you all got to play with Lego at some point, if not, I'll sit here and feel sad for a minute, as every child should have a Lego box to play with, it creates imagination, problem solving, building and all the wonderful things that life will need us to possess.

Pity party over, Lego, you take one brick at a time, you lay it and grab another and lay it next to it, once you have laid the first layer you start on the next, carefully overlapping the layers for a strong hold. As you lay brick after brick, sometimes thoughtfully, sometimes mindlessly, a building of sorts starts to appear, mine always turned into some sort of Castle, I dreamt big as a kid!

In this building you imagine a life that is lived there, you feel you have built a safe little area of your own, your building contains your world and the way you want it.

This is what I had achieved with all my 'Fine' bricks. Day after day I laid them down, I carefully overlapped the layers, making sure it was strong. The more people spoke to me the higher my building became, it even had a roof, a roof that finished my 'Fine' building, but it was dark in my house, why was it dark?

To let light in you need windows, I had no windows, I was too busy with the bricks. I realised I couldn't leave my house; I hadn't built in a door. Are you starting to see where I'm going with this?

I had built a house around me with no way of seeing the light and no way of getting in and out. I was stuck. What I find interesting now, looking back is that people couldn't see in, and people couldn't get in, just as my 'fines' stopped people from seeing what was going on inside my head. Depression gives you survival skills you never dreamed you had. So where from here? Well, let's face it, I was able to keep reality at arm's length, it gave me time to think about the next hurdle that came.

I built all of this with a smile on my face, with laughter at times, with overthinking, with no energy (yep, depression robs you of your energy, that's why I became fat!!) and I built it with a job lot of 'Fines'.

Then came in 'Em with her sledgehammer.

'Em is family on Grant's side, the similarities in our lives are almost unbelievable, but you can believe them as they are true. Married at the same age, same place as a honeymoon, same number of kids, same way of thinking, she only has to look at me in a certain way and I know exactly what she's saying.

I was also blessed to work with her in the years that were hardest, I survived work because of her. I don't know if she owns a sledgehammer but let's say she does, she knew that something was going on with me, that I had pulled back, I'd become a Hermit. (I thought they had long hair and long toenails, that certainly wasn't me, I keep on top of my nails!!).

I'd let out little bits when she asked, but wanted to save her from me, she had her own family, she didn't need the burden of me on top of that, she never made me feel like a burden, that's me overthinking again.

'Em respected my 'Fine' house but lifted her hammer and broke down a doorway so she could get in.

She saw I wasn't going to put a doorway in myself, she built one for me, so she could get in and I had a way when I was ready to get out.

Let me take you back to a night that helped me take the Fine bricks down and use them to rebuild a lighthouse.

I was standing in B&Q with Grant, in my gym gear, hair tied back, no makeup, choosing paints and buying filler and some kind of edging. He takes me to all the best places.

'Em text and said let's get together for dessert tonight, we can eat and talk. Now this is normally a great combo, but that night I couldn't, I couldn't face talking to anyone, and anyone that knows me, knows I love a good chat.

I said to Grant I really didn't want to go, I couldn't, I had tears in my eyes, my heart was pounding, I asked Grant to call her and say we were busy. He said no. I said please. He said No, I said Why. He said "I really think you need to talk with 'Em, I see I'm not the one to help you with this, but I think she is, I think you need to go".

I can't describe fully what happened at that moment, but Grant had found some cracks in my house, I was able to hear his voice clearly for the first time in a long time.

I stood in B&Q, still not wanting to go, but typing Ok, I'll meet you there in half an hour!!

Grant dropped me there, still in my gym clothes, I got there first, found a table and waited for a couple of minutes, my stomach was churning, my heart pounding, I felt agitated, I could easily have left, but something kept me there.

'Em was there soon after, looking fab, I still think she should have come in a bin liner! She asked how my day had been, I said Fine. She looked me in the eye and said she didn't want to hear fine from me again that night. I just want to take a minute here to acknowledge the steps taken from 'Em,

-she recognised something wasn't right, but didn't charge straight in

-she kept contact, always a love you at the end

-she listened to what I was saying without telling me I was being silly

-she made the first move of breaking down the wall, but then let me move at my own pace to come through it.

This is so important, my house wasn't built in a day, it can't be torn down in a day.

Back to the evening.

I can't recall the entire conversation but I do remember her asking questions, and listening to what I had to say, she asked what my feelings were, what I worried about, what was I overthinking, had I had darker thoughts, why do I feel no one loves me or wants me around.

She let me talk and her questions were led from that.

That was the first time I had said out loud that I had thought about taking my own life. It was a bitter/sweet experience.

I felt like a weight had been lifted just by saying, but it was now replaced by guilt that the weight had shifted to her.

That night I cried, I laughed, I talked, I thought, and came away knowing that 'Em was going to be there whatever.

She told me that the next day, I needed to call my Doctor and get an appointment. I needed to start the process of getting this sorted. 'Em dropped me home, hugged me and said, it's going to be ok, we got this.

I don't know if people completely understand how important follow-up is in life. It's essential to make things happen, in all areas of life.

It took me an hour to work up the courage to call the doctors the next day, when I did, I put the phone down and started shaking, I'd done it, I'd made that first step.

At the end of the day 'Em text to see if I'd been able to. That follow up text at that moment meant the world. It meant she cared.

I told her yes, I was scared stiff, I didn't know if I was ready but that I felt good about it. Which that in itself confused me as being scared and feeling good don't normally go together in my head, but the more I thought about it, it was anxiety building up in me... yep, let's throw something else into the mix!!

How does fear and feeling good equal anxiety I hear you ask? Well, it's a combination of fear and excitement, well it is in my case. When these two emotions come together it can cause all sorts of chaos within your mind.

An example. Pre-Covid we actually went to the church on Sunday mornings (we will after Covid, just enjoying the lay ins at the moment).

Now I would wake up, get dressed, eat breakfast, laugh with my kids, Grant was at church a little earlier due to meetings.

I was fine, and I can tell you now that as I write, the feelings I am about to discuss are coming back to me, see, depression and anxiety are a work-in-progress!!

As I ushered the kids out of the door to the car, the panic feeling set in, Do I look ok? Who will be there today? What if I talk too much? I know I bore people! I'll sit on my own at the back, that way I'll be ok! Don't forget to smile! Sliding into the car, sorting myself out, I'd be repeating in my head .... Smile, don't talk too much, I can do this... over and over again.

The ride to church was always ok, I'd pull into the car park hoping there'd be no one by the cars, my thought was that if I got there just on time or a little late everyone would be inside. The kids would pile out and wander to the entrance and I would always be behind.

There's a pathway that leads up, and as I stepped on the path and headed towards the entrance I could feel the panic growing, I would always pause at the door to calm my heart, and nerves, put a smile on my face and walk in to the pew and sit down.

Every Sunday this would happen, and I know that when we go back, I'll be the same for a while. For me, anxiety was not having control over things.

My life was spiralling out of my control, my eating was out of control, my daughter's diabetes was out of my control, I needed something that I had control over, and hiding myself away was something I could do. I controlled what and who I saw, it may have been a small thing, but it was something. I was in control of my house being built and who I let in (which ended up being no one, I've been brought up to be a better host than that!!).

Shall I tell you the reason I didn't go to the doctors initially... I didn't think he would believe me!

I thought he would just roll his eyes and say, yet someone else who thinks they have depression but is really just lazy. I did my Doctor a massive disservice. He is the most wonderful caring man. He has seen our family through some really hard times and still checks to see how we are. I realise that not everyone has a doctor like this, so I count myself blessed.

The car ride to see him was 10 minutes long, on my own and shaking like crazy, I could feel the tears starting already (no mascara, I learnt my lesson). I pulled into the car park and sat for a minute.

My head at that point… Nooooooo, I can't, he'll give me tablets, I don't want tablets, he's not going to believe me, he won't, he just won't. I don't want tablets; he won't give me tablets if he doesn't believe me.

I was a wreck. I think I'm normally quite a laid-back person (family might disagree) but this illness that had rudely entered my body without permission had turned me into someone completely different.

I got out of the car, it was dark and I remember thinking, how apt, I'm about to step into the light from the darkness of my self-built house (I'm quite a reflective person by nature).

Once I'd signed in on the screen, (we are very tech advanced at our doctors, touch screen, three taps and you're in), which I was actually quite happy about. This meant I didn't have to break down in tears in front of the receptionist. I didn't have to tell her I had arrived, and I was ready to start rebuilding my life.

I wasn't sat down for long before I was called in, I tentatively knocked on the door (manners always, depression or not) and entered into the room. My Doctor was sat there with a big smile on his face, his feet never reach the floor, something that really endears me to him. He put out his hand and motioned for me to sit down, I sat, smiled and said Hello. He looked at me, still smiling and said, "What can I do for you?"

More tears than Noah's flood!!! All I did was open my mouth and the tears flowed, I looked at him and said out loud for the first time...... I think I have depression!

I waited for the "Well I'll be the judge of that". Instead I got "Oh Keely, I'm so sorry to hear that, how do you want me to help?"

I don't know if I've ever felt so many emotions at one time. Let me share them, then tell me how you would handle them.

Relief, happiness, shock, disbelief, confusion, and pride. Pride in myself that I had finally taken the first step, disbelief that he actually believed me, shock, at his response, relief that I had finally released that sentence from my brain, Confusion that now what? and Happiness that he wanted to help me and help me quick.

You know when someone is trying to give you lots of information and you just don't hear what's being said, well my Doctor was very aware that I was in no fit state to take in an essay at that point.

He gave me two pieces of paper, a leaflet on depression, and a leaflet on counselling with a phone number.

I took them as he was explaining that he just needed to ask a few questions to find out where abouts on the scale I was.

I'm normally quite an open person, and I love a questionnaire to find out what kind of fairy you are, or what 80's sitcom character you are, but this one was different, this one was delving deeper into a place I had closed off to people.

He asked the questions, I answered the questions, he read the results... It's coming out as you have severe depression and severe anxiety!!!

Was I ready for that? No.

I like to do well on tests, that was the worst possible mark to get!! Also, that meant what I had was real and that the severity of it meant a lot of work, this wasn't a quick fix.

In today's world, it's a buy now pay later way of living. Get it now, worry about the hard work of paying it off another time. This wasn't part of that world; I can't get happy now and worry about how to keep happy later.

This was going to be hard from the beginning, it would require focus, honesty, strength and passion to get better. It was going to be a daily job, yes job, to cope with it, understand it, unlearn certain coping mechanisms and learn new ones, being prepared to lay yourself bare (not literally, that's just weird) to someone who is trying to help and make you better.

So yeah, I was gutted, but a little feeling deep inside kept rearing its head to let me know that this was going to be ok, tough, but ok.

I went to say thank you but instead blurted out "I don't want to take tablets". Thought Tourette's had been added to my list for a moment, but no, just my fear of becoming addicted to tablets. I do have an addictive personality, for three years I was addicted to the gym, four hours a day, and I am totally addicted to Hot Chocolate's, I need to see if I can find a help group to join, My name's Keely and I'm addicted to Hot Chocolate.

The Doctor almost seemed relieved that I had said it, he told me he thought I was right and that counselling in his opinion was the better way forward. See, completely blessed, I had a doctor that got it. If you feel your Doctor doesn't get it, change surgeries, you need a doctor that knows you and understands.

He suggested I call the number on the leaflet and see if I can make my first appointment. I'll come to the counselling later as there are two kinds, and I'll let you know why I went for a certain one.

I thanked him for being so understanding and walked back to my car, I just sat and cried for a minute, I think it was all the built up stress, anxiety, and worry flowing out of my body. I could physically feel my shoulders lowering, my heartbeat becoming normal, my head becoming clearer.

I had a plan, the plan was in the form of a line of numbers, and all I had to do was tap that sequence of numbers into my phone the next day and the plan was in action.

I went to bed that night exhausted, it had really taken it out of me, I felt like I had had the work out of my life, my muscles were all relaxing, so ached, my eyes hurt from all the crying, I was brain dead from all the thinking, but I felt a feeling I hadn't felt in a long time, hope.

Hope that life would get better, that I would stop feeling numb, that I would laugh more (I do love to laugh) that my mind would let me be happy, and let me start feeling worthy of people talking to me. It was only a little spark, but it was there, and I could feel it.

CBT, NOPE, NOT YOUR BIKE TEST!

I will let you know; I do have my motorbike license and I achieved it whilst having depression!!

You become a master at hiding things during this time, I achieved a lot of things while at the height of my illness, and as I look back I can remember there was no true joy about them, it was just something I had done, not including my parachute jump, that was freaking awesome.

What am I talking about when I say CBT? Well, let me enlighten you.

There are two types of counselling, The one we all think of, someone sat with you, either on a sofa or a couch, letting you unload everything from your deepest darkest past, and the other is a CBT therapist, otherwise known as Cognitive Behavioural Therapy.

It is completely your choice as to which one you will want to go with, I went with CBT, and I'll tell you why.

I read about both counselling techniques and each in their own ways are fantastic, but my strategies for coping needed to be un-learned. My thinking went like this...

If I go to counselling I open up Pandora's box and I have no way of coping with that, only going back to the ways I normally cope, if

I go with CBT, I learn new coping skills, I gain an understanding of what is happening in my brain, I learn about the bodies reaction to stress's that are put on it.

If I do CBT first, then I can learn how to cope with all the stuff that would come out in a counselling session. To me that made sense. Unlearn, Relearn, Cope.

So that's what I did. I called the CBT therapist and booked an appointment.

I make it sound like I just picked up the phone and did it. I sat for quite a while thinking of what I would say, of what she would say, was this the right thing (overthinkers anonymous, that's the group I need!)

The kids were at school and I sat at the dining table. Feeling like a kid who was being made to grow up. I didn't want too, this was a very adult thing to do, I was taking charge of my own life. It was going to be me trying to fix it, no quick fix plasters put on it. This needed stitches to keep the wound from re opening.

I spoke to the lady on the other end of the phone, and she informed me that there was an eight week wait for a therapist!! What!!! Where would I be at in eight weeks? What would the state of my mind be in eight weeks?

I'm not ashamed to say it, I got scared. I could now see what my brain was capable of, I wanted it fixed. Would eight weeks be too long to wait? What else could I do, I had to wait. I was no more important than anyone else trying to seek treatment, I would wait.

I got off the phone and randomly started doodling on a bit of paper laying on the table, now I'm rubbish at keeping a journal, and I'm not about to tell you that I became the most fantastic journal keeper in the world, but I did decide during doodling that I needed to at least try and keep some positivity in my daily thoughts during the waiting period.

My outlet is photography, I love to take pictures, and Instagram is a perfect way to keep a journal of our life without me having to write pages. So I decided to take at least a picture a day of something that made me happy.

This was my first solo step to me taking my life back into my control.

I must admit, it was a struggle quite a few of the days to find something to photograph, when you're in that frame of mind, it's easier for some reason to focus on the negative in life.

You may have nine positive experiences in a day and one negative, but you will focus on the one. It seems easier for the brain to make an understanding of the negative because that's what life is at the moment, dark, lonely, negative.

To think of a positive and try to apply it to your life is almost alien. My brain would be thinking "That's nice of you to say, but I know that people don't really want to be around me" It doesn't fit into the brain's way of thinking at the time.

This is my life, this is what my brain has told me, this is the truth, positivity is just people being nice, but not really true. That's the brain during depression.

So photography extraordinaire I became. Some days it was a made bed, other days it was my family, others it was a flower or sunset and others it was a cheese sandwich, but that made me happy.

I don't know about you, but I love looking back on photos, it brings me a sense of joy and calm. To look back now on what bought me happiness during those years makes me both laugh and cry.

I also think of how simple things gave me my positive moment during my day, and how lovely it is to be happy because of a sandwich!!

Looking at these moments is looking at my baby steps to regaining my life. It's me trying to rewire my brain to start believing that life is worth living, that I am worthy and enough to live this life. That life can bring joy. But that it can also bring sadness, but that's ok, sadness is part of life, but there are ways to handle it.

During these months, instead of rebuilding the wall that 'Em had broken, I built a small circle of people around me that I could feel safe with, that I knew I could talk to and it would stay with them, they wouldn't judge, they wouldn't take over, they were people that wanted me to move forward, to be there for me, to lift me when I started sliding down again, because your mind will revert back to the way it thought before, in the early days, it's hard to shake the darkness off, it's a constant battle. So to have people there to catch you and know when to catch is a life saver (literally sometimes).

I would say I had a lot more down days than good days while I was waiting.

One thing I forgot to say when speaking to the CBT team was that they asked me if I was okay to retake the questionnaire I had taken at the doctors, for their records, so they could see how great my need was.

They told me I was bumped nearer to the top of the list because of my results. This felt like I was being told I was being put nearer to the top of the line at Costa's because my Hot Chocolate was getting colder quicker than others. I never jump the queue, but if someone rehomes me closer to the till, I'm happy to oblige.

I still had only told three to four people what I was going through, and some days had to really push myself to verbally communicate what was going on in my mind. I will tell you though, that talking is therapy in itself.

People may not be able to help, you may not want advice, but talking through your thoughts can prioritise the things that are really worth worrying about.

To get it out of your head is to clear a little space in your mind.

There's a 90% chance you are going to fill it again with something else negative until you learn new ways to work through and replace with a new way of thinking.

I received the call to say I had made it to the top of the list and would be allocated my own therapist.

The hard part that I was able to hide away in its own little box, was about to begin. The box was about to be opened. I had to give myself a pep talk to not put that box away and pull out another that might be nicer to work through.

I said thank you, we worked out a date and time for her to call back, mainly for pleasantries and a get to know each other. On the NHS you get 6 free sessions. God bless the NHS.

The first session is the get to know you, retake the questionnaire, (you get to know the questions off by heart, as you will take it quite a few times for them to be able to gauge where you're at) and what you expect to achieve in your time with them, this I neglected to mention is all done over the phone.

I found this easier as I felt I could relax in my own home, she didn't know who I was apart from my name, and I could really open up because I wasn't face to face with someone staring at me. That's kind of awkward.

The first session I sat at my dining table, with paper and pen, with an empty house around me. Paper and pen I have no idea why, I wasn't told to have them, I was so used to turning up to a meeting at work with them that I think I did it instinctively, so I used them to doodle as I spoke.

Lesser known fact, doodlers are said to be more intelligent then non doodlers. I knew that because I am a doodler.

I retook the test. Out of 27 I scored 25.

I'm rubbish at maths, but even I knew that that wasn't a good score. I know the saying is 'The only way is up', for me the only way was down, and that's the way I intended to head.

I wasn't sure how or what it included yet, but I knew that this lady (who I'll call B) was going to put me on the right path at least.

I felt somewhere in the middle of ok and good coming off the phone. I think I wanted her to say, I see, this is your problem, this is how we fix it, but she didn't.

I see now it gave us both thinking time to understand what I was about to undergo and for her, to think of the best course of action, I had a couple of weeks in between each appointment, this gave me time to practice and master the techniques she was teaching me.

The brain is a complicated, wonderful piece of engineering and you can't begin to understand it in five minutes. People spend a lifetime studying this intricate array of wires flowing around an enclosed bone bowl. I really don't think I've mastered my brain in six, one-hour long sessions, but it gave me a start on understanding what goes on and how we can begin to change our thoughts and reactions to thoughts.

Let me just say, I am no professional. Remember that I am someone that has gone through and is still trying to conquer this illness.

The things I share are not from any PHD I might have acquired (I haven't) but from the way I see things, the experiences I have gone through, and the reflection I have taken in trying to deal with this. Who knows, one day I may be the world's greatest brain scientist (chances looking slim) but for now I am happy to share and give an insight as a real-life Anxious depressive!! Ha-ha

So many wonderful things go on in this world, so many lovely people cross our paths, so many experiences define our existence on this earth. How do you deal with them?

Some would embrace them. Things such as hugs, meeting up, girly dinners out, conversation. Some would be wary at first but then run towards them with arms open.

Others, like myself before all of this, go running towards them, arms open, rugby tackle them to the floor and love the life out of them. What felt so natural suddenly became very scary.

Things that happened in the world, even though I had no control over them, (and if I did would make no difference), were a major deal and added another weight to my heart. It was another thing I had to think about. I handled this by not watching any news. It weighed me down if I did.

People that crossed my path… well they couldn't, I had dug up the path and made a Mote. As I explained earlier, it was easier not to interact, and the experiences were definitely defining me, but not for the good.

A little sneak peek into the mind at that time… I thought I was becoming strong, I was controlling who I spoke to, what I did or didn't do, where I went, I had built a fine house by myself, that takes strength!

I had completely mixed up the need to be strong and the need to in control.

To be honest, I think I still get a little confused even today, but I have the insight into my way of thinking kindly given to me by my CBT therapist. She showed me that my feelings were valid, I wasn't being silly, that I wasn't the only one dealing with this, that she was there to work through this with me, however long it took.

She showed me not a new way of thinking, but reminded me of my old way of thinking, she gave me the tools to be able to access that part of my brain that had been taken hostage and locked away by the depression. She was giving me the key to unlock it. What a cheesy line…. She gave me the key… but I don't think I could have picked a truer statement.

My old way of thinking had been locked away (in a very ornate treasure chest), I couldn't or didn't even know how to unlock it. Did I have the key? … I didn't even have a door to my house, let alone a key to my treasure chest!

So, she gave me a key, the key that would hopefully unlock an understanding and in turn a 'new' way of thinking.

I was excited but nervous, you know when you're going through a cardboard box of Christmas decorations from the garage, they've been there all year, just tucked away in a corner, all taped up, but when you get it out and open it up there's always that fear of a mouse jumping out (I have a major fear of mice, I was bitten by a field mouse as a child, traumatised for life). I give you this example only because it has happened to me, the fear was real and so was the mouse that jumped out. I almost died.

There was definitely a fear of opening up that chest, I wanted to get out the better way of thinking, but what if a nasty memory jumped out (mouse came in handy for an analogy) what if because of that one thing I couldn't go near the box again.

That thought laid heavy on my mind after that first session. Although I had laid some of my burden on to B, I wasn't sure I was ready for any surprises, although are bad memories surprises? I think they're just more like experiences that have got comfy in the corner of the box, and when disturbed by removal of things, naturally fall or jump out.

We don't fear happy memories falling out onto us do we! Who knows, I may get some of those fall out of the chest. Once I was comfortable with this, I began to look forward to my next session.

I may have to find a counsellor for my fear of mice though, that's still going strong!

I won't take you through each session, but I will give you a summary of interesting and thought-provoking times that came.

One thing I did do with each session was sit in the same place every time.

To me this was comfort, it was calm, and it was consistent. I would sit on my bed, looking out of my window, my gaze falling on nothing but trees. I'm at my calmest in nature. For me this gave me privacy and a calming space to talk.

It worked well. I'm a talker and I love to just sit and chat with friends and family, I had decided that if this was to work, I needed to love the chat. B was easy to talk to which made things a whole lot easier, I wanted to be open, I had been closed for so long, but it took courage to do that.

The weird thing is though, whilst having the guilt of passing a bit of the burden onto family, I had no guilt about passing it to her.

When I said goodbye and clicked off the phone, there was no guilt, only a sense of release, awareness, and towards the latter sessions, determination.

When you live with guilt for so long (talking about being a burden to others, or so I thought) to be able to talk to someone and not come away with guilt is an amazing experience. You feel you want to talk to this person forever, they understand and not only understand, they seem to melt the guilt away during the conversation. They are magic. It's not a trading time, as in emotions and feelings.... I'll share my burden of sadness with you but now I have the burden of guilt to replace it. There was no replacement.

I can only liken it to this. Over the past year we have renovated a house, gutted it and started from scratch. It's been hard work, tears, aches, and changes made. I have made so many trips to the rubbish tip, that they are starting to recognize me. We take all the rubbish from the house and dump it in the containers, as I drive away I feel lighter, I feel I can go back to sort through some more bits from the house, the next trip feels lighter still, until you get to a point, that all you need is the small black bin in your garden to throw things away. When we first moved to the area I didn't know where the tip was, so I asked, and someone told me, all very polite and lovely.

This is what having a CBT therapist is like. That light feeling gets better every time you say goodbye. Knowing that you've taken it to the right place to dispose of, you know that as you walk away, things are less crowded in your head, the clutter is being cleared, you can return knowing that certain areas are free from the piles that have been building up, and it's a welcome feeling, a new feeling, one that's gives you hope.

So knowing this, you can now understand how over the weeks I looked forward to my sessions with B, having put the fear away, and got a glimpse of how I could start feeling, I loved 2pm telephone calls.

When you start to open up you realise that this is what you've been craving for a long time.

Someone to just sit and listen to what's going on inside your head, not even to understand it at first but just listen. You have a sudden awakening to the art of communication, someone is actually going to willingly allow you to pour out all of the contents of you head, and not even recoil in disgust and judgement. (if that was literal, I'm not so sure about the disgust!!)

It was refreshing. No guilt, that's what was refreshing, I know people would want me to talk to them, but the guilt was associated to them, no guilt with B.

It was hard to unlearn.

Think about trying to unlearn how to do a certain exercise. You've been doing it that way for a few years, then someone who knows quite a bit about that exercise says to you, I understand why you're doing it that way, but if you did it this way it's less stress on your body and you'll get bigger benefits from that muscle.

You're thinking… great! I'm up for less stress and bigger benefits. So you take their advice, you start to implement it into your training, goes great for a couple of times then you slip back in the old way of doing it.

You realise and correct yourself; you keep slipping back quite a few times till it becomes habit. I had to unlearn my brains thinking pattern.

That's even harder as you can't watch yourself do it in a mirror and notice your incorrect posture. It's hidden and only you know what it's thinking.

It's extremely easy to slip back, to have those thoughts reappear, which is why it's so important to have that contact with whoever is helping you, because they may see or hear what you can't.

So, yeah, unlearning was hard, and it was exhausting sometimes trying to keep on top of it, but once you have thought your way out of a moment of darkness, you want that again. You begin to like the feeling of taking control in a positive way. At first you don't recognise the signs of darkness approaching, so you feel like there's a constant battle in your mind, you know what you need to do, but it appeared without a heads up, so you're firefighting the whole time.

As the sessions go on you start to learn what the triggers may be, to recognise when those feelings are creeping in, to be able to put strategies into place rather than keep firefighting. I'm not going to say it gets easier, as I still have days I struggle, but they are far less.

I would say that you are able to deal with daily life better. Where food shopping was a big ordeal for me, it's part of my life now, I just do it. (still hate it, it's boring right!) I've started to enjoy the art of conversation again (probably to my family and friends dismay, I don't shut up) I still think I am boring people, and I'll to reign it in, but it doesn't keep me from being with people anymore.

The one thing I have come away with from CBT is that our mind is a gift to be looked after.

It contains information, memories, both sad and happy. It can get sick, but it can be treated. What we put into it, will be what we get back from it.

It's amazing but ever so fragile, therefore we need to take care of it. It is the instrument that literally keeps us going each day.

PLACES

This section is the one I've not really looked forward to. The feeling in my stomach right now is oh so familiar. I can feel the confusion starting to creep in (apologies if nothing makes sense).

Have you ever thought "Do they really want me here, or was it a pity invite?"

Have you ever thought "I'm a burden"?

Ever thought "People really don't want me around" "They're only talking to me until someone better comes along"

Has it crossed your mind more than once or 10 times "It would be better for others if I wasn't here"?

Now when I say, 'wasn't here', I'm not talking about going home, I mean not walking this beautiful earth we have. Remember earlier when I was talking about darkness? I've never been in such a thick darkness in my life. Depression is tactile. What do I mean by this?

Imagine laying in your bed at night, you're so tired from fighting the day, you think surely, you'd fall straight to sleep. This is when depression puts its fancy shoes on and goes to town. Laying in the quiet of your bedroom (well quiet all bar Grant's snoring), thoughts start creeping into your mind.

These thoughts aren't the usual 'Must do that tomorrow' 'Flip, I forgot to do that' 'Must call so and so in the morning', these thoughts wear black, they hide in the shadows but make their presence known. You can feel them start to enter your mind, you try to keep them at bay, but they keep creeping, working their way along the paths of your conscious, and as they go, they drop little pebbles of doubt.

Not only do you have this activity going on in your brain, but you also have what I like to call the Cloak of Depression. This cloak you will not find in any store, it is not wanted by the rich and famous, you won't find it online, but you will find it on the backs of many people.

The cloak is heavy, during the day it weighs heavy on your shoulders and at night it weighs heavy on your heart. When I used to lay in bed, it felt like a heavier duvet had been laid on me, I found it harder to breathe, well to get a deep breath, that's what I mean about it being tactile. It affected my senses, but the interesting thing, as I look back, is to see how it also distorted my senses. Let me elaborate.

It affected my sense of sound – people were telling me they wanted me around, they loved me, I was worthy. I heard the opposite.

It affected my sense of sight – People smiled at me, they invited me, they texted me. I saw pity.

It affected my sense of touch – I didn't feel worthy of affection, or even want it.

It affected my sense of taste and smell – it didn't, I just had to write them to finish the list!

Let me give you an analogy......

Grant has a weighted vest, he uses it when walking at the moment, but it can be used when doing any kind of physical activity. The purpose of this vest is to add extra weight for body weight exercises, be that walking, running or agility.

It increases the intensity of the activity or exercise being performed; it even helps with bone density. It's fantastic in helping with strength, cardio, and endurance. Which is sounding like a win/win situation at the moment isn't it! When you add mass, it can influence the way your muscles deal with the stresses and strains. When you add the extra weight, you are using more force, more energy to perform the task, this in turn leads to faster energy depletion.

I looked up to see what the outcome would be of wearing a vest such as this all day, here's a summary of what I found: If you were to wear the vest all day long it would be likely to cause soreness, tiredness, muscle burn in the neck, shoulders, lower legs and lower back.

Mmmmmm, if I wore it all day it would cause these reactions, I was wearing that weighted cloak all day every day, and do you know what, they're right. It does cause that, along with sore heart, and an extremely tired mind. So, I read what to do if this should happen…Take off the vest!!!!!

Let me go back through this and really get it lodged into your mind here.

The weighted vest is obviously the cloak of depression. I was wearing it for walking, running, driving, cooking, working, everything I did, it definitely increased the intensity of every task I performed, whether large or small (I was surprised some days at how I actually got anything done with the extra weight).

Not sure about the state of my bones, they're still holding my skin in shape so pretty happy there. The weighted vest affects your expertly made muscles that flow through your body, the cloak affects the expertly made ball of muscle that resides in your head.

The added weight will cause stresses and strains on these muscles, extra weight on the muscle. In my case, the extra weight in my mind was, as we read above, causing faster energy depletion. (hope I've made sense so far).

What was interesting was that my brain was tired, but that made my whole body tired. The body is a wonderful thing, through all of this I have gained a greater respect of my own body and the creator of it. The brain is the link to all that happens inside us: if the brain is tired, or has a muscle soreness, then guess what, the rest will follow.

So, the answer to all my problems if I were wearing the vest... Take it off. Simple.

Guess what... Taking off that cloak is not simple. You don't have the energy to untie the bow, let alone take it off (cloaks with bows are always fancier, Velcro just won't do it).

So you sit there, with it draped round you, watching other people almost float around, seemingly weightless, (I say seemingly, as I am well aware that we don't have freshly polished windows, showing into each other's lives). Wishing that someone would see you struggling to take it off, but at the same time not wanting that sudden exposure.

Although the cloak is heavy, it is a protection, but a protection from what?

Most days you would give anything to get away from the negative thoughts in your head, but yet you can't seem to find the energy to even flip a corner to poke your toe out. So, if you're inside the cloak, with negative thoughts, where's the protection?

The protection comes in the form of a distorted thought. It's not protection for yourself, you believe you are protecting others from you. If you stay within the confines of the cloak, people won't notice you as much, they'll start to forget you, they will eventually stop asking to help, and there you are, you have saved them from your brokenness being heaped upon them and becoming a burden, because that's how you come to see yourself and your 'problems'...a burden.

The mind is a weird and wonderful place, it can take you from euphoric feelings to the darkest places you didn't know existed.

What does the title of this section 'Places' have to do with what I'm talking about? This is where I hope I can keep the balance of reality and light heartedness going. My heart is actually pounding as I skim my fingers over the laptop. I really thought I had worked through this and it was done and dusted. Lesson learned, the past never disappears, it needs to stay to be learned from.

Have you ever had a thought that's popped into your head that made you think 'woah, keeping that to myself, don't think others would understand that' or a thought that brings such sorrow to your heart that you just don't want anyone else to have that sorrow in them?

These are the thoughts that start to formulate in your mind, when you are down that hole and you can't even see any light, when the cloak is heaped heavy on you as you lay in bed trying to sleep.

These thoughts are thoughts that come to you, and stay within the recesses of your mind, always there, never shared, but build in strength every time they come. I still find it hard to write it, let alone say it out loud.

I always found it funny (light-hearted moment) that these dark thoughts would mainly come in the darkness of night. When you're in the dark, that's what your thought pattern becomes. I can liken it to a street.

During the day, dangers and negative things don't seem as bad, you can see the path before you, you know what to avoid, you can see what's coming towards you. In the dark on the same path, the path is less visible, you can only see a few steps ahead, you can't see around you so you think danger is closer, it gets bigger in your mind, a little fox scurrying across your path has now grown into an escapee Lion, that's hungry. The dark in my experience enlarges things, so negative thoughts are going to become soul destroying thoughts.

So with Grant's dulcet snoring tones carrying in the air, my brain would awaken the nightly ritual of overthinking the day, of thoughts of doubt, thoughts of self-loathing, and thoughts of taking my own life (Phew, said it, I still find it so hard to talk about, it carries such a sense of guilt).

When this process begins, it starts with one little throw-away comment someone might have said, such as, "That's great, could you just add that to it for me, thanks so much".

Reading that statement does it seem positive or negative? Now, sitting where I am in life, I can say positive, but to a person with depression and anxiety this is completely negative.

What bit do you think we will focus on? That's right, 'can you just add….' Forget that they've said that's great, they've told me I got it wrong, I forgot to put in something and it's not right, they've seen it, they know better, I should have known to put that in, it's wrong!

Can you see how things get escalated so quickly, and that's just one thought, try overthinking the whole day!!

As the night progresses, you lay there, the thoughts in your head becoming bigger, becoming a problem, and then Bam, the answer… You're the problem, all these things have happened, and you are the common denominator.

Then you think, how do I deal with this problem, "if I wasn't here, the problem wouldn't be here" "People's lives would be better if I wasn't here, I cause problems" "How would I do it?"

A little warning, things are about to get a little dark for a mo.

Suicide – there, the word is out there.

People don't talk about it a lot as it's uncomfortable, but it's a real word, it's a real action, it's real life.

Do you know the sad thing about the first time I thought about it, I wasn't even surprised. It seemed the natural course of action. How awful is that! Things aren't right, I'm the problem, I'll kill myself.

Very blunt and to the point. That was how my brain told me the problem could be solved. Every time they came back, they grew in strength, laying foundations in my brain and building on top, a solid structure, a firm plan. Night after night of thinking, knowing the problem was me, then coming to the same conclusion on how to fix it. It then progressed to not only thoughts of taking that step but how and where? How would I do it? Where would I do …. Places.

I hear from others that people who take their own lives are selfish. Let me give you a little insight into what they may be thinking before that dreadful moment happens. Guilt, fear, heartbreak, confusion.

Guilt because you know that what you're doing will have ramifications on the family you leave behind, how can I do this to my husband and children? Those poor people that find me.

Fear because you have no idea what death is like, you see it as an end, but practicalities come into it. Will it hurt, what if it goes wrong and I'm left with horrendous life-long injuries, what if I change my mind at the last minute and it's too late?

Heartbreak because you know what you're leaving behind.

Confusion because you're not sure if this is the right thing. It makes sense to you, but would it cause more problems?

You go through all of this and yet still your brain tells you this is the best course of action.

I had three places picked out, two away from our hometown, and one randomly in our hometown. This one in a way was the easier of the three options.

I won't go into where's and how's as I really don't think that matters, but I will say that one of the places has been demolished, so don't have to think about that anymore (one thing off my over-thinking list!). It is amazing to me now, thinking back on it how real it was. That it was seriously a viable option for me.

I can honestly say since completing CBT I haven't had those thoughts.

I realise how toxic they were, but at that time it seemed a reality. I didn't go through with any of these plans, the ways I had picked out were not elaborate, they were relatively easy to do, they just needed the courage to do it. When it came to it, my family meant more. I couldn't and didn't want to leave them. They became my focus.

You know when you make memories, and you're in the moment, appreciate that time but take pictures of that moment and write down where you were and how you felt.

This became a way of coping with days that crushed me. I love my family, I love photography, I love words, I love making memories, I love travel, when all of these loves come together, I'm grabbing that moment in time and keeping it in my mind's treasure chest for when I need them. You soon start to figure out lifelines. It may be different for everyone, I'm definitely a memories person, I love making them and looking back on them.

Once I had learned these new skills from my CBT therapist, I started to build a new house. One that let in light, one that had a door to invite people in so I could show them the new way I was building, I was using bricks of memories.

This house though, the more I used my new skills and coping techniques, became more of a summer house. I didn't need to live in it, I was able to spend more time in the family home that we had all built.

When needed on certain days, I can take a wander to my personal house and recharge. If people came to visit, they would knock, and I was in a position to invite them in or ask them to come back later.

I continue to have this house, and I continue to add to it. I don't let crowds in, I've only had a few visitors other than family. This house tells the truth, of who I really am, of what's really important. That life although hard at times has always been there to be lived and enjoyed, whether it comes with tears or laughter.

There will always be memories to look back on and learn from. If you were to enter my summer house, you would come across a coffee table (every summer house has to have a coffee table). On it you would find my book of life. In this book of life, you would flip through the pages and notice that it is a mixture of happy and sad.

Why keep the sad? I would explain to you that this is how my life was woven, into the tapestry it is becoming. I see the dark cord, and I see the light, I even see gold, and they're not woven in blocks. They are placed side by side, overlapping each other. You may get more dark colours in one area than another, but if you look closely you will still find some light.

As you stand back, you begin to see the bigger picture unfolding. You begin to notice that the dark areas were surrounded by light.

This is my life evolving, this book is a book of learning. My memory house, reminding me of overcoming, of fun and of love.

WALKING HAND
IN HAND

Who loves holding hands?

I do, there's a connection between the two people involved. An unsaid understanding of…. I won't let you go; we'll walk this path together. A state of happiness is in the air.

Let me just put a different slant on that for you, sorry, I hate to ruin a moment.

What if the person who is holding your hand is someone you want to be a million miles away from? Is there an air of happiness? Is there a feeling of safety?

Being on the other side of CBT, I feel the cloak has now been removed from me, but put onto a being, whom it's fits, they don't seem weighed down by it, they don't seem concerned by it. This being has now become depression. They've grabbed my hand and told me we are going to walk this path together. It's not a path I chose, it's certainly not one I want to continue on, but I'm being told, 'I won't let you go; we'll walk this path together'.

How different one sentence can sound when presented in two different ways.

I don't know if it's an overactive imagination on my part or my brain's way of making sense of things, but by having depression become a being, it made it more real, but also easier to deal with. Something that I can identify with, something that I can reason with. I know that a few CBT sessions aren't going to make it all go away, and it will stay away forever. Mistakes will happen, old ways of thinking may creep back in, so I have to be prepared for that, I have to know and be ok with this thing that may always be in my life.

I used to lay in bed sometimes during the worst of it, thinking it would always be with me, this monster, that towered above me, not being able to control the decisions it makes, not being able to reason with it, just walking the path it had chosen, and being dragged along.

But CBT taught me differently. It taught me I wasn't the only one on this path, yes I was the only one holding it's hand, but people are dotted ahead, and behind, that I can look to when this being called depression starts making the decisions.

I can look to these people for the strength and confidence to be able to say "No, this is the way we go, this is the speed we walk, this is the way I think".

I often had a picture in my head of a child holding a monster's hand, (it kind of reminded me of Sully from Monsters Inc.) walking away from me. The child would look up every so often, then turn back it's gaze to the front. I think of this now and really identify with the child, meaning I look at depression, I know it's there, I'm aware of it, but now having the tools and knowledge I do, I don't look all the time, that's not all I see. I now have the strength to turn my head forward, to see the path ahead, to see the beauty that is around me, and the people that are mingling on the path.

There may be little potholes in the path, there may be times when you lose sight of the way ahead. I know the old saying is 'Don't look back, you're not going that way', but sometimes you may have to take a quick glance back to remember who has been stopping you from falling backwards, who has been there, arms open in case you fall again.

I would say to become more aware of who surrounds you, who catches you, who shows up on your path. These are the people that will keep you walking straight and will not allow you to be pulled off.

Can I say I'll never have to worry about coming off the path again? No, I can't. I can't see into the future, and I can't manipulate future circumstances to fit in with me.

What I can do is embrace the future, I don't have to necessarily go running towards it with open arms, but I can be happy to see what it may bring. I can build my strength up.

How? Bodybuilders, they lift weights daily to strengthen the muscle to make it bigger, to then be able to lift heavier weights. A mental gym session is needed. I have taken to Yoga and Meditation.

I cannot begin to express the deep sense of wellbeing this is starting to give me. Especially the meditation. I do both in my gym at home. Yoga starts my calming process, seeing where in my body needs work, the gentle fluid movements are a balm to a sometimes-tired body. Then onto my mind workout. When I say workout, I'm not straining my mind in any way, That I leave for Maths.!!. I just do 15 minutes after yoga, and I come away feeling totally relaxed and rejuvenated. When they say you feel at peace, they're not lying. I find doing it in the morning helps me set up for the day. I go into the day calm, there may be things that rile me throughout the day, but I'm in better frame of mind to deal with them.

Meditation is not only helping your body relax, but also helps your mind to relax, to focus, to heal.

I had a moment the other day that made me really focus on my own existence. Whilst focussing on my breathing, it hit me that breathing was the only thing keeping me alive. I know, a basic primary school knowledge, but it really hit me because I was so focussed on what was keeping me here on this earth. A tiny breath, something that we take for granted every day, something that we do without thinking. Once you take the time to ponder on the one thing, you realise how wonderfully made you are. That one tiny breath is what keeps your body getting what it needs to function.

It made me realise that one negative tiny thought took me to a place that I couldn't be alive mentally. I was focussed on a thought that wanted to take me out of this earth.

Thoughts are something that happens naturally throughout our day, right? We have millions of things running through our mind every day, and I don't even know how many we latch onto during that time, but when we focus on a thought it becomes something. We have the power to focus on either the negative or positive.

We have the power to push a negative thought along (I like to use the word along and not away as I see when you push something away, it will come back, laws of nature, but when you push something along, you are pushing it along on its journey, it doesn't have to stay in yours, hence push along, and not away). That thought doesn't need to reside in our mind, it didn't have an invite, let the bouncer do their job and turn it away.

I can only say I have the power now, I couldn't have said it six months ago, I can say it because with the love of others I took the first step into the mental gym to help strengthen what had become weak.

The mind can be a crazy place, it can be scary, it can be amazing, but ultimately it's what you make it, if you feel like you have no power, ask for help, ask for help, ask for help.

I cannot stress it enough, I really wished I had reached out earlier to save the years of heartache and darkness.

So when all these things are put together, CBT, strength, awareness, daily meditation, and focus, you begin to realise that not only are you holding hands with depression, you are holding hands with a long line of people that are saying, " We won't let you go, We'll walk this path together".

WHERE TO NOW

To be honest, I'd love Bali, Italy, anywhere with a gorgeous beach, but we all know that's not what I mean, and I have to say, I honestly don't know.

I have a mixture of days. I have a lot more good days than I used to have, but as I knew I would, I do get the bad days too. The day's I'll make an excuse as to why I can't come, the days I struggle with thoughts and emotions.

I have made steps in inviting friends and family that I once pushed away, with the 'I'm fine' shield, back into my daily life. To share in each other's time, laughter and love. I have started to make a plan of how to get my life back, be it fitness, social, adventure and knowledge. Writing this book has been a way of therapy as well as raising awareness and helping to explain what family and friends may be going through, or indeed yourself.

It's allowed me to reflect on the past few years, what has actually happened in my life, the good and the bad. It's made me think of times and seasons, thought patterns, actions and reactions, the world in which we live. In this time of pandemic too, it's given me the opportunity to really step back from things and see what's truly important.

Mental health is so important.

It's the thing that helps build relationships, understand life, keep your body functioning, understand emotions, and gives you your personality and character. There are so many factors that can affect it but knowing how to handle these factors is vital.

Knowing how to strengthen your self-worth is a priority.

Learning to how to love yourself and accept others love for you is lifesaving. Taking your time to learn how to do these things will give you the power to overcome the battle that is depression, it will give you the insight to the true you and in turn will give you the insight into others.

I can't see what the future holds at the moment as I am taking it one day at a time, working on the areas of my plan that will allow me to enter the next phase of my life and recovery.

I have started to talk to others that have shared my........ I'm not going to say journey, for some reason I really don't like the phrase, 'It's been a journey' So I will say…. have shared my experiences in some form or other. It's quite eye opening to hear of others stories. At first you feel guilty you were not there for them, but then there's a sense of true understanding.

The moment you realise that this person understands the emotions you have felt, and they are still here, living their life, using the coping techniques that you yourself are now using, and saying to you 'I understand', and do you know what? They really do.

All I can say is the future is what I choose to make it.

It really is. Good, bad, dull, exciting, full or empty. That's my choice, I may feel a little tug from my constant companion on my path, but that's ok, I'm not the only one on the path, and I know that now.

The only fine houses I want to build now are real life ones with Grant and the kids, and filling them with memories, with plenty of windows and doors to allow friends and family to enter in and share life with us. Sounds cheesy I know, but I've missed that, I loved being around people.

I've grown up surrounded by people, sometimes I would come home from school and my Mum had brought some random person home for dinner because she knew they wouldn't have any that evening. A trait which I love in her. I love the richness of human differences, the diverse opinions that bring out conversation, the different outlooks on life and situations. So to not have that has been weird, and not me. To be able to catch a glimpse of what used to be is like a refreshing drink after days of not drinking.

It makes me happy to think that this way of life may come back, with work from me and a desire to bring that life to reality again, that the relationships I started to pick apart will eventually be entwined together again. But this will only come about if I work on the knowledge I have acquired.

Life isn't easy, but it's worth it.

If I had to go through this to understand what truly matters, then it was worth it. I would rather not have gone through it, and if I hadn't learnt anything from it, what a total waste of life and years it would have been.

When you are at your lowest, sometimes the only way to look is up. Believe me, I looked up quite a bit, pleading for help. Whatever or whoever you believe in, I believe I was heard. So to not take this knowledge forward with me would be a waste, applying it into my life now can only make the future a little easier to comprehend and achieve.

I don't know where I'm really going from here, but I know it won't be boring.

What I do know is that there will be day's when I need someone, and there will be day's that I've got it. It's good to recognise that, to be able to say that asking for help is NOT weakness, it's knowing where your weakness lies and knowing that asking for help is a strength. That's so important to know the difference.

I know that life is a gift, and gifts are meant to be enjoyed. I know that my mind and mental health need to be looked after and not pushed to the bottom of the list.

Life is about looking after each other, it's about making sure we reach out to those in need, to give love, service, time, food to those who are in need.

The one thing we need to remember is that we cannot give if we ourselves are empty. This does not mean the world revolves around us, it means we need to watch our internal gauge and if we see it getting low, we take a step back for a while and let other's look after us while we recharge. Then we are good to go again.

I hope with all my heart that this book has given you an insight into what many people deal with daily.

I hope that it has given you understanding and compassion.

I hope that if you recognise any patterns or traits within yourself or others that it has given you the courage to make that first step.

Life doesn't have to be hard; it can be healed. My heart is aware of sorrow, but it's also aware of peace.

I pray that one day peace will be in the heart of all.

ABOUT THE AUTHOR

Keely Watling

 Keely has a passion for family, travel, and the great outdoors which all feature regularly in her photography. She likes life to be varied, whether that is skydiving, ballroom lessons, or recently passing a motorbike test.

In her career, Keely has been a Beauty Therapist, mother of six, primary school Learning Support Assistant, and a one to one for young children with Autism, Attention Deficit Hyperactivity Disorder, Attention Deficit Disorder, Oppositional Defiant Disorder, and global development special needs. She has embraced the different personalities and challenges that came with each role (including being married to Grant).

Spiritually, Keely's Christian faith and beliefs have helped her throughout low times as well as high. She has found peace in this, in the practice of Yoga, meditation, and being in nature.